Prayer, Praise and Worship:
A Guide to Everyday Living

Craig Morrisey

Craig Morrisey

Copyright © 2014 Craig Morrisey

All rights reserved.

ISBN: 978-0692279311

PREFACE

As I grew up in life and church, I started to understand and see things very differently. I saw how easy it was to get sidetracked and distracted with power, influences and the gifts in which God has blessed you with. At one point in my life, I myself got distracted because I forgot that it was about God, people being blessed and not about me. As people in ministry have been placed in power, it is very easy to get beside yourself. As I started preparing my self for music workshops, I saw the need for people to get back to the basics. That was going after God first and then perfecting gifts and talents. That's how this guide was birthed. us understanding how prayer, praise and worship play an important part in our growth spiritually, mentally and physically. These three things play a vital role in our relationship with God and how we live in the world. Not only did I want to help push people in the direction of knowing how important your relationship with God is; I wanted people to see the importance of knowing your purpose. And the importance of using your gifts and talents to build the kingdom of God and ministry. I know there are many other things that you can use to help with these things, but these are the things I want to focus on. I pray that after reading this, you will see the importance of your relationship with God and the balance that you need to be effective in your everyday life.

Prayer, Praise and Worship: A Guide To Everyday Living

Craig Morrisey

CONTENTS

Acknowledgments i

1 Understanding Your Purpose

2 Prayer

3 Praise

4 Worship

5 Having Your Leaders Heart

6 Prayer, Praise and Worship In Perfect Harmony

Craig Morrisey

ACKNOWLEDGMENTS

I thank God for this opportunity to write from my heart about the issues I have been seeing in the body of Christ. I realize that without His anointing and guidance, I would't be where I am today. I am thankful for the gifts and talents He has blessed me with. It's a privilege and a honor to be used by God, for His glory, to help people. I would like to thank my Beautiful wife Crystal Morrisey. Thanks for believing in me and pushing me through the rough times where I couldn't see or hear what God was saying in my life. You have been very instrumental in my life changing and growing for the better. And for that, I Love You from the bottom of my heart. I thank God for my mom. What you have taught me over the years, will never leave me and I will always cherish it for the rest of my life. To my family and my church family, thank you for your continuing love and support over the years. For the people that helped me prepare this manuscript, THANK YOU!

CHAPTER 1

UNDERSTANDING YOUR PURPOSE

Purpose: The reason for which something is done or created or for which something exists.

Knowing why you exist or why you were created is the first step to maximizing your potential that God has placed inside you. We were all created to be different, but created in (God's) image. Genesis 1:26

There was and still is a specific reason that God the Father, the Son and the Holy Ghost took counsel to create us. The main reason in our life for living is for God to get the glory out of our lives.

When we understand that totally, we will see life very differently. God getting glory out of our lives is what we should strive for everyday we live. One of the best ways we can give God glory in our life is to live out our purpose.

When we were created we all were given gifts and talents. If you are reading today,

you believe the ministry of praise and worship, songs or musicianship is a part of your

ministry to give God glory.

This ministry in the body of Christ is a key element in getting God's message to people.

Your singing and minstrel gifts have the power to transform atmospheres and allow God to come and dwell in the midst of the people. It has the potential to transform the lives

that come to church to seek God's presence. In understanding your purpose of this ministry, you have to go back and look who and was the first person in charge of changing the atmosphere and ushering in the spirit to allow God to flow. It seems crazy to some people to see that God wanted someone to give out a sound, a distinct sound that would enable Him to flow in a vain, that would unlock the mysteries of God.

Lucifer

Before he was cast out of heaven, Lucifer was created to be the chief worship leader. Before any artist ever thought about singing praises and worshipping God, Lucifer, meaning "morning star," was created to bring about a sound that couldn't be compared to anyone. His whole job was to create such a worship that even God Himself couldn't resist to lose Himself.

Lucifer's Purpose

According to Ezekiel 28:12, Lucifer was the sum of wisdom and beauty, meaning he was perfect in God's eyes concerning these things. Ezekiel 28:14 lets us know that he was anointed and created for a particular task and service (Worship). He had the task of setting the stage and the atmosphere of worship and praise unto God. Lucifer was allowed places that the other angels couldn't enter all because of his purpose.

Your purpose will allow you in a place of God that others can't go. That's why it is so important not to take your purpose for granted. In order for us as minstrels of God to stay effective, we must stay in the place (presence of God) that God has openly let us roam freely because of our purpose. It's in the presence of God, the throne of the almighty One that allows us to tap into what He (God) wants.

Ezekiel 28:13 lets us know that Lucifer was well equipped with everything he needed to do his job, which was to lead the angels in praise and worship to God. When God chose us and anointed us for this propose (created us for this existence) of leading praise and worship and ushering in God's presence, we were well equipped to do the job. We possess the tools and attributes of God to perform the task. We can't flow if we don't understand our purpose behind our ministry of music unto the Lord.

It's purpose that defines us; it's purpose that unlocks the gifts and talents within us. When you understand your purpose, it causes you to stay in your lane. You won't try to become something or someone you are not. Purpose allows you to know that we are skillfully and wonderfully made in God's image. We DO NOT have to try to copy someone else's worship style because God has given each one of us our own style of worship to Him. Purpose caused Lucifer to maximize his created potential in God. He understood it was his job to create worship to God like no other. It is our job to discover our purpose and maximize it to its fullest extent. It is when we start maximizing our purpose that God gets all the glory.In maximizing your purpose, your life changes because shift to a place of leadership. Whether you are the minister of music, praise and worship leader, musician, singer on the praise team or choir, it puts you in a place of leadership. This is a place that should be considered sacred, and not a place of spotlight or place of showmanship. When you understand your purpose, you realize that its not you doing what you are doing; it's God working through you. It's God's anointing enabling and equipping you to lead. Understanding your purpose helps you to stay in a place of reverence to God, so that you can continue to be used by Him. Understanding your purpose helps you stay where God has placed you. STAY IN POSITION!

Stay in the position of humility.

Stay in the position of openness.

Stay in the position of gratefulness.

Stay in the position of being able to hear from God.

These are some of the keys of being effective in the music ministry.

CHAPTER 2

PRAYER

Prayer: a devout petition to or spiritual communication with God. Direct conversation between you and God.

Prayer is a key ingredient to understanding your purpose and being effective in the area God created you to do. There are many prayers in the Bible that we can look to for learning how to talk to God and understanding his heart. Your prayer life has to be stronger than your time you spend trying to master your craft. Whether singing or playing instruments, your prayer life has to be the most important aspect of effective ministering through music and song.

I Thessalonians 5:17 "Pray without ceasing."

When you pray to God, you don't want to get into a religious mode of trying to copy someone else's prayer. Nothing bothers me more than when I talk to people and they try to talk and act like others. Ironically, I wanted to talk to them to get to know them and who they tried to impersonate. It's the same way with God. When we pray to God, we are talking to Him directly. God wants you to come to Him as who you are, not someone else. It is prayer that's going to help you understand the mind and heart of God.

Proverbs 3:5-6

As musicians and singers our minds and should always strive to understand the thoughts of God. Everything we do in ministry comes from knowing what God wants and needs from us. As minstrels, its our job to understand God's heart, so it is displayed it through our praise and worship.

As psalmist and minstrels, we know that God has given us gifts of singing and playing. We must never rely on just our gifts and talents to be effective in the body of Christ. Prayer helps us seek the face of God and is needed in order to get wisdom, revelation, understanding and anointing to truly be effective in ministry.

David's Heart

David is a main character in the Bible who understood the heart of God. He knew the importance of prayer to God in his everyday life. David understood that as long as he stayed in direct contact with God, he would get to know God more intimately than ever before. David was a man who God declared was after his Heart. Besides David being king, he was a skillful musician. He understood the importance of the anointing of God.

When Saul was vexed with a spirit, he immediately told his men to find someone who could play skillfully on the harp so his spirit could be at peace. His men immediately thought of David. They were looking for skill, but they didn't understand that it was the anointing that destroyed the yolk.

That's why it's important to keep a prayer life constantly open to God. His presence causes the anointing to be evident in your life. David knew that because in Psalm 51:10-11, he prayed to God and asked God to create in him a clean heart and renew a right spirit within him. He went a step further and said "cast me not away from your presence and take not Your Holy Spirit from me." David knew in order for him to fulfill his purpose and to walk rightly before God, he needed to have a clean heart. As singers and musicians, we must strive for this. "Sin" separates us from God and when we are separated, we can't flow in a constant vain while fulfilling our purpose and that purpose is to usher in the presence of God.

It is our purpose as psalmists and minstrels to have a prayer life for constant growth in God. As time passes, the world changes. We have to be in direct contact with God on how to reach each generation. Prayer unlocks the door to the mysteries of God. It's in God that we need for each season and time in our lives. We must constantly seek the face of God in order to stay tuned into the times we are living and stay tuned into the flow of praise and worship.

This comes into play when you are seeking God for songs to minister to Him and the people of God. When they called David to come play for Saul, he had to be tuned to what God wanted to hear and what God wanted him to play to drive out the spirit. As praise and worship leaders, ministers of music, music directors and those in leadership, this is very important. We have to get out of picking songs because they sound good. You need to get songs that will touch the heart of God and the people. Prayer will help you understand what needs to be sung and what you need to hear. We are doing this unto God, so what better way to please Him than to find out what He likes.

Prayer unlocks that door to His heart so you can find what sends up a sweet smelling savor to God's nostril. Prayer causes you to not hit and miss doing praise and worship. Prayer causes direct flow of communication between you and God even during praise and worship. Prayer causes us as psalmist and minstrels of God not to become prideful and arrogant because prayer helps you understand that if it wasn't for me seeking God and asking Him to minister through me, I couldn't do what I have been purposed to do.

Pride

Pride is one thing that the devil tries to use to destroy the music ministry in church. The devil understood that pride is what got him kicked out of heaven and the reason he lost his job, which was to provide true worship and praise unto God. Pride is a feeling of pleasure from one's own achievements. It's one thing that God can't stand. When you become prideful, you begin to think that you are the reason ministry goes the way it goes. You begin to think that you are operating on your own and not needing assistance from God to minister fully. This was the mistake Lucifer made when he started thinking that he could do this on his own. He thought he was the main reason that the ministry of praise and worship was flowing like it was supposed to be.

Truthfully, some of us as praise and worship leaders get this way. We have an opportunity that satan didn't have. We have the right to pray to God and ask for forgiveness. Satan didn't have that right, so that's why he hates us as worship leaders and psalmist and minstrels because we can pray to God and get like David and ask for a clean heart. Ask to be purified and cleansed. Pray to God that He doesn't take his Holy Spirit away from you. It's a dangerous thing when you don't pray to God for forgiveness and continue to stay in your prideful ways. Proverbs 16:18 states "Pride goes before destruction and an haughty spirit before a great fall."

It's a dangerous thing to think you don't need prayer time and you don't need one on one time with God because you got this. You are setting yourself up for a big fall if you don't humble yourself and turn from your wicked ways. II Chronicles 7:14 tells us to "Humble yourselves and PRAY, and seek my face and turn from their wicked ways then will I hear from heaven and will forgive their sin and will heal their land." We have a promise that when we get off track that if we humble ourselves, understand that it's not about us, that we need God in everything we do and pray. This lets us understand how important it is to pray and seek the face of God. Prayer helps you see yourself and not other faults first and then turn from your wicked ways. Stop thinking its all about you. Stop the perverseness of the spirit. This is another way that the enemy tries to corrupt the music ministry by perverting it, causing your praise and worship to be tainted.

The devil understands how important the praise and worship ministry really is to God, so he tries to pervert the people of God so they won't give true praise and worship unto God with the confusion of sexuality, promiscuity, whoredom, etc. The devil's job is to keep you from being genuine and not worship God in spirit and in truth. The devil knows that's the only way to be effective. God says that if you would stop all these things, don't live one life at home and then try to live another life in church, but let worship be your life style on a daily basis, then God will hear from heaven and will forgive your sins and will heal your land, your very being and soul. Prayer is so important to the body of Christ as believers. As psalmists and minstrels, we should try to perfect having a prayer life before we try to perfect our skills to sing and play unto God. Through prayer, it helps us understand how to praise God.

CHAPTER 3

PRAISE

Praise: the expression of approval or admiration for someone or something.

Just as we spend time in prayer, we should take time just to praise God. Psalms 150 is very clear on how passionate we should be about praising God. There should always be a praise on your lips, no matter what the circumstance or outcome. We as believers must always be thankful. Being thankful to God is something that we must convey everyday of our lives. David lets us know that because we have breath in our bodies and that should give us enough reason to praise God. He specifically says "Let everything that has breath praise ye the Lord." We as a people should take it as a command and always be thankful and grateful unto God. As praise and worship leaders, singers and minstrels, we should set times during the day when we just tell God how thankful we are to Him. There should be times when we just break in a praise just to let God know that there is no one like Jehovah. Acts 16:25 said, "Paul and Silas prayed and sung praises unto God. And by them praying and singing praises, a great earthquake happened which shook the very foundations of the prison. And then it said immediately all the prison doors were open and everyone's hands were loosed."

This lets us know that as singers and minstrels if we take time out everyday to pray and sing praises unto God, not only will it affect our life, but others. When we pray and praise, it's a powerful combination. God is trying to get us to see that when praise becomes who you are, you can shake the very foundation of the thing that is trying to hold you captive. However, not only your foundation, but when you come for service to minister through music and songs, you help shake the foundations of the congregation. Not only you will be free, but you will help loose the bonds and chains that had the people of God in bondage. That is what we are called to do as we usher in the presence of God through praise and worship.

There is a distinct sound that goes off in the atmosphere when you release praise unto God. The Bible lets us know that there are angels who sit around the throne and sing praises to the almighty God all day long. They are so in awe of His presence they can't help but to praise His name. As believers, as good as the angels sing praises unto God, we have a song that the angels can't sing. We can shout from the mountain we have been redeemed, bought with a price and that the blood that Jesus shed for us changed our whole life. When we open our mouths and begin to sing praises unto God, it does something to Him that the angels can't do. When God looks at us, He sees His son Jesus. As we praise Him, He sees His children praising Him. Because God is better than any earthly father, when we praise, it makes God want to get off His throne and move heaven and earth just for us. When you praise privately, that spills over in public, so that when you open your mouth or play the instruments, that same praise fills the atmosphere in church and it causes God to come sit right in our presence. Psalms 22:3 says "God inhabits the praise of Israel" (His people). Inhabit means "to live or dwell in a place," so when we praise God, we cause God to come live and dwell right where we are, and when God shows, change has to take place. It's important we praise as often as we can. When we praise God, everything around us that's not like God, has to change. If He dwells in our praise, anything not like Him can't stay. In other words, praise produces positive change in any situation, because God shows up when we praise. It is so detrimental to you as a praise and worship leader, singer and minstrel to always praise God in all things. Your praise has the power to change not only your situation, but the situation of those that surround you such as our family, friends and your church congregation. Again, what you do in private will spill out in public. If you praise God at home, you won't have a problem praising Him anywhere else. David says in Psalm 100:4 "Enter into His gates with thanksgiving and into His courts with praise; be thankful unto Him and bless His name." If we, as apart of the music ministry, come into service with praise on our lips (because we didn't wait until Sunday or the start of a service and praise God during the week), the atmosphere in church will not be hard to set because praise can't help but to spring from our lips. It would be a life style and not just a time to sing; it would be ministry in its highest form unto God and His people. Praise is a powerful weapon, if we use it right, the power of change could be limitless in not only our lives, but everyone we have the opportunity in which to minister. Use your praise to allow God to live where you are and bring positive change to every situation and your everyday living experience.

CHAPTER 4

WORSHIP

When we get praise inside of us and is evident in our lives everyday, this is true worship. Worship is not just a church thing that we do, but it's a lifestyle that we live that's pleasing to God. Worship is something that must come from the heart and not be made in any kind of way. John 4:24 says, "God is a spirit and they who worship Him must worship Him in spirit and in truth." This scripture lets us know that we must be able to tap into the spirit with our worship. The first thing we have to do in order to do this is to make sure that sin is not evident in our hearts. This is not suggesting you have to be perfect, but there must be a free flow unto God and sin blocks this. We as leaders, singers and minstrels should daily examine ourselves to make sure nothing is blocking us getting intimate with God through worship. Many times, we forget to check ourselves to make sure there is nothing hindering the flow of God, and it causes the worship from us to be stagnate and not be acceptable unto God. It doesn't matter if it's a big sin or little sin, as we like to categorize it. Sin is sin and it will cause a separation between you and our heavenly father. It is detrimental to our flow that in order to be effective in our ministry, we make sure that we seek God for His cleansing power daily.

Worship: the reverent love and devotion accorded a deity, an idol, or a sacred object. Ardent devotion; adoration.

We as believers should constantly worship all day long. Not saying you get fired on your job because you refuse to work because you say must go worship. I'm saying this because you reverence God and love Him so much that everything you do should be done unto Him all day long. That's true worship. One definition says that worship is to honor, and one way to honor God is to keep His commandments in your heart and to make sure that we don't shame His name. Because we confess Jesus as our Lord and Savior, everything we do will be looked at differently. People will judge us on a higher standard. They will expect different things from us than they do the world, so our lifestyle must be a constant worship unto God.

As psalmists and minstrels, worship is a real important aspect of our lives. When we worship God, we loose ourselves in Him and it causes us to see Him in a way that we have never seen before. When we worship, it allows us to see how messed up we are and that as good as we think we are, we don't have it all together. Worship keeps you humble because it lets you know and realize that God is the reason we are who we are. Just as we should take time out to pray and praise, we should always take time out to just reverence God for Him being God alone. David realized that no matter the accolades and achievements, it was nothing that he had done, but it was because of God's anointing that kept him in a place of prominence. He understood if he wanted to reach God and stay in His presence, he must go after His heart. Worship pulls on the heart strings of God. There is nothing like it, for God to hear His creation cry out to Him, just to tell Him how much we love and adore Him. How much we need Him and can't live without Him. That's true worship when you understand that everything I am and hope to be comes from God and He is my creator. It opens your heart up to tell God nothing can take His place in your hearts.

True worship causes God to unlock the mysteries of Himself for us. It causes God to reveal Himself in such a way that it leaves us thirsty for His presence. It causes us to develop a hunger and thirst for God that only God can satisfy. For instance, if you were real thirsty, you ever notice that the more sodas you drink, the more you become thirsty, but if you ever get a good glass of water, it seems like your body grasps for it with everything with in you. Well that's how it is with us; sometimes we try to fill our thirst with everything else besides Jesus. We try to make excuses why we don't have time to get into the presence of God. I guarantee you that if you ever tap into the presence of God, the quenching that you will feel is indescribable. It opens a whole new world unto you that opens your eyes so that you can see clearly. It causes the cares of this world and the things that hinder us to not bother us, because nothing can enter with you in worship that is not of God. Worship allows you to escape whatever is hindering you, blocking you and causing you to fill depressed and limited. That's why as leaders in the music ministry and psalmists and minstrels, it is our lifeline to what God wants in our life daily. When we worship we cancel out the plans of the enemy. When we worship, we cause God to come see about us in a expedient manner. Worship causes us to get to know Him (God) and to know what His plan is for our lives. That's why it's vital that we spend time in worship because we need God every time we minister to be evident in our lives. When you worship in your home or wherever you choose, it will be easy to tap into God's presence when you minister for the Glory of God. Because then its not an act, its not fake or a put on. Your worship is not important just for you, but it's vital for all the people in which you minister. The saints are depending on us as the music ministry to usher them into the presence of God. If we say that God has called us to minister through music and songs, we must take it serious enough to make sure we are in a place were we can change the atmosphere so that God can be worshipped in spirit and in truth.

A songwriter wrote, "I worship you almighty God, for there is none like you." We must get to a place that we realize that our worship destroys the plan of the enemy and cause God Heart to move on our behalf when you worship, it takes you to a place of serenity and peace. It allows you to get to know God on a one on one basis. When we get to know God like that, it will be endless possibilities and opportunities that God will get the glory out of our lives.

One of the best forms of worship unto God is obedience. It is very important to live a life of obedience unto God because obedience will open doors up for the glory to be present in your life. One definition of worship is to honor. What better way to honor God and His word, but by obeying Him? Psalm 37:3 says, "The steps of a good man are ordered by the Lord and he delighteth in his way." Obedience to God through your worship will allow God to point you in a place that you will be able to usher the spirit in when you minister. Your everyday life should be in constant obedience to God. Our life is to represent God in every way here on earth. As we reverence God, it makes us want to please Him. It should be our goal everyday of our lives, that God can use us to get glory for Himself. This is not just on Sunday or what day you come together to give God praise, but 7 days a week should be constant worship for God. Everywhere we go, the world should see something different in us. Those in it may not know about God, but they should be able to tell a difference in their lifestyle and your lifestyle. Your obedience to God, not just practicing good moral acts, but true obedience should separate you from the world's standards and God standards. More than us being psalmists and minstrels, we are salt and light to the world (Matthew 5:13-14). Our lifestyle of worship should influence someone else to want to know what I must do to be saved.

With us being salt to the world, our obedience should add flavor to the world. In a world bland and full of darkness, we should add instant flavor that changes the appetite of the world to make those in it want what we have instead of wanting what they have always known. We know that food without salt doesn't taste well, but when you add just a pinch of salt, it changes everything. Just a pinch of salt changes the whole dish. That's what God has called us to do and that is to bring positive change to this world. By being a light, it lets the world see how to honor God. Through your constant obedience, we shine our light everyday in a world full of darkness. No matter how dark a place is, one piece of light stands out. Luke 8:16 tells us "Not to hide our lamp or our light under the bed but to put it on the lamp stand to light the whole room." With our obedience, we show the world how to love and worship God. When we don't try to hide who we are, but show our appreciation to God by honoring His word, that's true worship unto God.

CHAPTER 5

HAVING YOUR LEADER'S HEART

Romans 10:14 "And how are they to believe in Him of whom they never heard. And how are they to hear without a preacher."

This is a key part of any ministry in the church in order for the ministry to flow and flourish in the pursuit of the Glory of God being fulfilled. Your Leader (pastor) is the Gift who God has given you in order for the commandments and direct instructions from God be sent to you. The reason that we know this is because Romans 10:15 says "How can men preach unless they are sent?"

It's the pastor's assignment to make sure he or she is hearing correctly from God to provide you with the instructions you need to live your life in purpose. The pastor takes his or her assignment very serious because he or she is responsible for souls being saved, grooming for spiritual growth and helping provide the body of Christ the hope (Good News) of Christ Jesus. If the pastor takes his or her assignment and responsibility seriously, we as singers and minstrels also should. There should be a connection in the spirit with every part of the ministry with its leader, especially the music Ministry.

Music plays a vital part in the service because before the pastor gets up to preach, the music comes first. The music that is sung or played should build a stage or platform for the preacher to release what God has given him or her. The songs sung should align with what the pastor is going to release to the people of God, but how can we know this if

(1) we are not tuned with God and (2) we are not tuned with our leader.

The Flow of the music ministry should always move in the vain of the leadership of the church. Some people may disagree, but I ask a question. How can the pastor release one thing from God and the music say something totally different? Is the leadership is missing God or the music ministry is missing God. As minstrels, it is our assignment to make sure we are not missing God and that we are portraying what our leadership is delivering on a daily basis. When you know you have a pastor who is laboring and his or her primary goal is to make sure the people see God and get to know God in a deeper way, then there should be a direct correlation between you as minstrel and the pastor. There should always be a building and a constant climatic flow in every service you attend so that when you as singers and musicians release the sound that God has given you, it should set at stage that the people of God are ready to receive the Word of God. When the pastor preaches, it should flow right from where you left, and not him or her spending time building the people to receive the word. When that happens, we as singers and musicians have failed at our assignment.

Many times we forget about the importance of being spiritually connected to our leadership. We choose songs because they are popular and the hit song to sing instead of seeking God for the songs that align with the Word that God wants to release that day. You as the music ministry must be so tuned with God and your leader that through praise and worship, God's word is released. When the pastor comes to speak, the power God is overshadowing the service to the point that nothing can be said. We have to take our assignment very serious and take our spiritual connection with leadership just as seriously.

It makes my mind think how David's men were so tuned with him. They understood David had a plan and it was their assignment to help David's plan flourish. They understood that David heard from God and he wouldn't let them go astray. They dedicated their lives to help him bring about God's plan for their lives; we have to do the same thing. We have to believe, trust and be on one accord with our leader to help the vision that God gave them come to pass. We can never get lost thinking it is all about us. This is about the

Kingdom of God and us helping God's will be done in earth as it is in heaven through the vision that God has placed in our leaders. Our music must portray that when we open our mouths to sing and when we play. It is for God's Glory to be revealed.

Seeking God helps us as worship leaders understand the direction of our leadership and what is trying to be accomplished. Every ministry is not the same in the approach it takes to release what God is saying, so it is key to have a spiritual connection with your leader in order to help carry out the assignment that God has given him or her. The ultimate goal of every leader is the Gospel of Jesus Christ is preached, souls are saved and the building and training of disciples to spread the Gospel around the world. What we do as the music ministry is to help them release what God is saying for us to hear by releasing a sound that makes preaching and ministry flow effectively.

CHAPTER 6

PRAYER, PRAISE AND WORSHIP IN PERFECT HARMONY

When we practice these three: prayer, praise and worship, they should bring about perfect harmony unto God. Don't get me wrong, we should practice our crafts and take time to master our gifts from God daily. More importantly, we should live a life full of prayer, praise and worship. When that happens everyday, when its time to minister through our music, an explosion should happen unto God. Now, you are not just singing songs to move the crowd or singing songs because they are current. Now when you sing songs, you can connect with the song. Understand the song and then relay the message when you minister to usher the presence of God. That is our job in ministry and that's to usher God's presence. We should not want a service or outing without the presence of God. What good is it to sing songs, get the crowd hype, but the spirit of God never shows. That's like everyone in the audience is moving and dancing, but God is on the front row asking when is it going to be about me? When am I going to be glorified? When we take time to make sure we are praying, ask God for His heart. Ask God to purify us so we can bring forth His word through the music. When we are singing, it is God's breathed word coming to life through song. We should always make sure we are praising God constantly, to make sure that we keep a grateful heart unto the Lord. We should constantly be thinking of things in which we can thank God. Knowing the gift we possess is not our gift, but it came from God, therefore we are grateful and thankful unto God that He chose us to usher His presence.

Make sure we are worshipping. Make sure that we are taking time to get intimate with God on a consistent basis. Make sure nothing else has our attention in a deeper way than God does and that we live a life of total obedience unto Him. If we as psalmists and minstrels take time to do these things with understanding unto God, as we minister we will see miracles, signs and wonders during praise and worship. Healing shall take place, yolks shall be destroyed and chains shall be broken when we live a life with prayer, praise and worship working in perfect harmony with each other. Follow the Word of God for your life and fulfill every assignment that He has placed over your life, so at the end you can hear Him say well done thy good and faithful servant. As we walk in our purpose, our life shall not only be an example, but we should allow God to get the glory out of our lives no matter what.

ABOUT THE AUTHOR

Craig Morrisey was born in Warsaw, NC and now resides in Morehead City, NC. At a very young age, music and leadership were instilled in him. He spent his years growing and striving to cultivate his gifts, talents and relationship with God in order to help bless this world. He has always had a passion for people, helping them get closer to God and to walk out their purpose in life. Craig is the Minister of Music of Tabernacle of Praise International Ministries, were he strives to relay the message that it is more important to have a relationship with God than to try to perfect your gifts and talents. He travels to conduct various workshops and engagements to spread the message of growth in every area of people lives. It's his passion to see everyone grow in their relationship with God, themselves and ministry. He is the husband to Crystal Morrisey, who he loves, adores and have grown together with for almost 9 years. He knows that with God, family and ministry, there needs to be a balance, and if you keep God the center of attention throughout your life, your drive and focus can continue to grow and build a foundation that changes this world for the better.

www.ingramcontent.com/pod-product-compliance
Lightning Source LLC
Chambersburg PA
CBHW061304040426
42444CB00010B/2505